"Al Jaffee's *MAD* Fold-In combines puzzle with great perception, and he will forever lay claim to this unique art form because I doubt that anyone will ever possess the genetic equipment required to reproduce it! Like Al himself, his work is one-of-a-kind."

—Lynn Johnston, creator of
For Better or For Worse

"I have yet to successfully reconfigure one of Al Jaffee's *MAD* Fold-Ins. This is not Al's fault, but rather a reflection of the fact that I never graduated from M.I.T. On the other hand, my four-year-old grandson (who *did* graduate from M.I.T.) readily bends and folds the pages in exactly the right places, shows them to me, I explain the gag to him, and we both laugh ourselves silly."

—Mell Lazarus, creator of
Momma and *Miss Peach*

"Al Jaffee's Fold-Ins easily surpass the ordinary, everyday brilliant cartoon features. Fold-Ins are ingeniously devised, brilliantly accomplished, hilariously funny, and they're all done by hand. Al Jaffee is one of the great cartoonists of our time."

—Arnold Roth (the other one), cartoonist,
Punch and *The New Yorker*

"I have always been amazed by Al Jaffee's genius in making his *MAD* Fold-Ins meet at the right place. I can't even fold a T-shirt, let alone make it come out with a different picture and funny joke line. Where does one learn this great science: Fold-In school?...Chinese laundry?...Road map company? It boggles my easily boggled mind. Excuse me. My *MAD* Fold-In book just arrived and I have to go practice."

—Mort Walker, creator of *Beetle Bailey*

"Al Jaffee's fame, I suspect, is largely tied to his wit and the 'interactive' fun he brought to the back cover of *MAD*. But what additionally amazed *me* was his sheer artistry. Forget folding the damn thing—just look how this guy could draw! The dilemma was always this: Very slowly and carefully fold the back cover of an issue of *MAD* magazine *without* creasing the page and quickly look at the joke. Jaffee's artistry— *before* the folding—was so amazing that I suspect I was not alone in not wanting to deface it in any way."

—Gary Larson, creator of
The Far Side

"How can one lucky guy be so talented? Al Jaffee is, just like his work, a true original. His FOLD THIS BOOK! is uproariously funny and totally unpredictable. Each page is a hilarious new surprise. My fingers are sore 'cause I couldn't stop folding! I don't know how he does it but I hope he never stops. Here's to Al Jaffee, one of comedy's greatest natural resources, from his longtime fan."

—Stan Lee, creator of
Marvel Comics

"When I was an adolescent, there were few things that gave me more pleasure than wrestling with Al Jaffee's inspired origami. Today, I find the same pleasure in watching my own thirteen-year-old do the same. To parents today, Jaffee and his merry cohorts at *MAD* are no longer subversive; they're merely indispensable. Who better to awaken our children to the world's foolishness than the very same gang of idiots who raised us?"

—Garry Trudeau, creator of *Doonesbury*

MAD
FOLD THIS BOOK!

A RIDICULOUS COLLECTION OF FOLD-INS

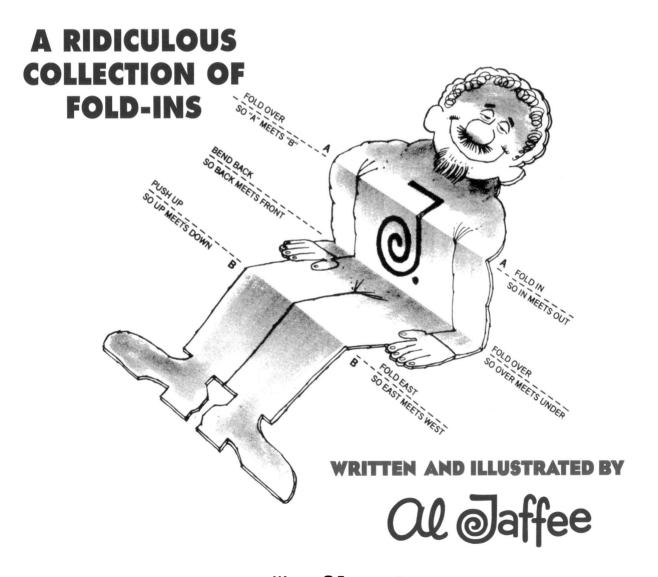

FOLD OVER
SO "A" MEETS "B" — — — A

BEND BACK
SO BACK MEETS FRONT — — —

PUSH UP
SO UP MEETS DOWN — — — B

A — FOLD IN
SO IN MEETS OUT

FOLD OVER
SO OVER MEETS UNDER

B — FOLD EAST
SO EAST MEETS WEST

WRITTEN AND ILLUSTRATED BY
Al Jaffee

Warner Ⓦ Treasures®
Published by Warner Books
A Time Warner Company

DEDICATION

To *MAD* editors Al Feldstein, Nick Meglin, and John Ficarra, who deserve a great deal of credit for the success and long life of the Fold-In, and to publisher Bill Gaines, who always backed us up.

A great big thank you to *MAD* art directors John Putnam, Lenny Brenner, and Jonathan Schneider for guiding Fold-Ins into print; to Charlie Kochman for dreaming up and following through on this project; to Amye Dyer for making the book happen; and to Michael LeGoff for his Fold-In article in *HOW* magazine.

And to my wife, Joyce, who has helped me enormously not only with this book, but also with individual Fold-Ins through the years.

MAD, Alfred E. Neuman, The Boy's Head Device logo, and all related indicia are trademarks of E. C. Publications, Inc.
Compilation and all new material copyright © 1997 by E. C. Publications, Inc. All Rights Reserved.

Warner Treasures® name and logo are registered trademarks of
Warner Books, Inc.
1271 Avenue of the Americas
New York, NY 10020

Ⓦ A Time Warner Company

Visit our Web site at http://warnerbooks.com

Visit *MAD* Online through AOL, keyword: MAD. For a free *MAD* online starter kit, call 1-800-203-2600.

Though Alfred E. Neuman wasn't the first to say "A fool and his money are soon parted," here's your chance
to prove the old adage right—subscribe to *MAD*! Simply call 1-800-4-MADMAG and mention code 5BKD1.
Operators are standing by (the water cooler).

Printed in the United States of America

First Printing: October 1997
10 9 8 7 6 5 4 3 2 1

ISBN: 0-446-91212-3

FOREWORD

After thinking about this for a long time, I am convinced that Al Jaffee's problem began when he was small. He probably did his homework on paper that should have been in a loose-leaf binder. I think what happened was his dog chewed up the binder so he had to fold his homework and tuck it into a pocket. Things like this can become a terrible habit and carry over into adulthood. Al is fortunate, however, in that he draws wonderful cartoons. Actually, Al can cartoon anything. No one admires his work more than I. We are lucky to have this collection of Fold-Ins. They are a lot of fun and perhaps inspiring in a unique way. It has occurred to me that we all have real-life problems that are separated like Al's cartoons. There must be some way to take these problems and fold them in the center. I'm sure it would work and I'm going to begin trying it.

Charles M. Schulz

Charles M. Schulz

INTRODUCTION

The concept for the Fold-In first occurred to Al Jaffee over thirty years ago as a response to the triple foldouts that had been very popular in magazines at the time. Jaffee explains, "*Playboy* had a foldout of a

beautiful woman in each issue, and *Life* magazine had these large, striking foldouts in which they'd show how the earth began or the solar system or something on that order—some massive panorama. Many magazines were hopping on the bandwagon, offering similar full-color spreads to their readers. I noticed this and thought, what's a good satirical comment on the trend? Then I figured, why not reverse it? If other magazines are doing these big, full-color foldouts, well, cheap old *MAD* should go completely the opposite way and do an ultra-modest black-and-white Fold-*In*!"

The idea of competing with those other, more impressive, first-class counterparts by offering a less-than-coach-class extravaganza had the typical self-deprecating *MAD* spin. The editorial staff, amenable cohorts to many of Jaffee's zany proposals, responded favorably. And a Fold-In by Al Jaffee has appeared on the inside back cover of almost every issue since *MAD* #86 (April 1964). Not bad for an idea originally conceived as a one-shot!

MAD readers were delighted with this new "puzzle," welcoming, perhaps, a more intellectual, sophisticated edge to balance the otherwise broader, flat-of-the-sword approach that remains the

---

How It's Done:

1. Each Fold-In starts with a pre-made grid. I begin by playing with different ideas that come into my head.

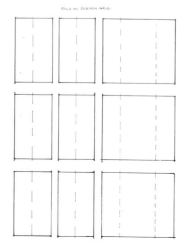

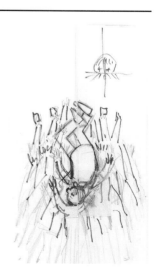

2. Once I arrive at a workable concept, I make quick thumbnail sketches of the folded picture. In this case it's a moshing "victim" being tumbled by a wild crowd of rock'n'roll enthusiasts.

magazine's hallmark. Mail poured in. When the volume is exceptionally large concerning a particular satirical piece, the *MAD* editors take note. If the response is positive, we regard it as a primitive guide and usually agree to continue to explore that area. If the feedback is especially negative, we ignore it. *MAD* objectivity has its limits!

Judging by the response to that initial offering and the nearly three hundred that have followed, the Fold-In has been established as one of the magazine's most memorable features. At first, no one was more surprised than Al Jaffee himself at the Fold-In's astonishing acceptance by *MAD*'s loyal readers. Through the years Jaffee has felt particularly gratified to learn that the first thing many *MAD* fans do upon buying the latest issue is turn to the inside back cover. There they try to figure out the pictorial puzzle without resorting to actually folding the page, much like doing a crossword puzzle without taking a peek at the solution. Mutilated collections of the magazine's back issues suggest that Jaffee has stumped readers more often than not. This delighted *MAD*'s erstwhile publisher Bill Gaines no end. He knew serious collectors valued pristine copies and therefore might be tempted to purchase an additional issue—one to read and fold, the other to keep in mint condition for posterity!

Jaffee, on the other hand, had ambivalent feelings about the feature's success. It was tricky work, and having to problem-solve the mechanics of each painting with a deadline hovering over his head issue after issue was nothing he had anticipated when first submitting the idea. However, as every subsequent Fold-In proved to be at least as successful as the

(a)

(b)

(c)

3. I copy the sketch onto a folded version of the grid (a). Then I separate the two parts (b) and roughly work out the piece by filling in the middle section (c).

previous one, he was easily conned by *MAD*'s editors into producing yet "one more" paradigm for each issue.

And so it continued for thirty-three issues, until 1968, when *MAD*'s printer offered Bill Gaines the opportunity of full-color reproduction on the inside covers at a negligible increase in cost. Gaines, believing the esthetics of his spartan package would be upgraded a notch by this additional use of color, approached Jaffee with the prospect of continuing as a full-color feature what heretofore had been black and white.

Immediately seeing the visual problems inherent in such a change, Jaffee came close to bailing out. He hadn't exactly found the make-one-into-two-separate-visuals concept especially easy to create, even in black and white. Matching the two end portions of a Fold-In (the center disappears when B is folded over left to match A) would be almost impossible in full color, he feared. Hiding a celebrity's face, for instance, when given only white, black, and the full range of gray to work with was more a challenge of manipulating shapes and forms than anything else. Drapery with a design pattern and billowing folds of one gray value can camouflage half the likeness on the right side, while bushes and foliage of the same gray value on the left might provide the other half of the face. Since the gray values of both sides are the same, they can blend seamlessly when the right and left halves are joined. The visual solution, the *new* image, won't challenge the reader's eye with inconsistencies. It's another matter entirely when the same scene is executed with a full range of color, matching the drapery with the exact hue and value as the green foliage in an attempt to produce that same hidden-face fake-out.

"Color isn't questioned in nonobjective painting," bemoans Jaffee. "But when realism is called for,

4. Here I design my central image, refining both the position and the expression of the moshing "victim" so that he'll work out when split in two and blended into the larger scene.

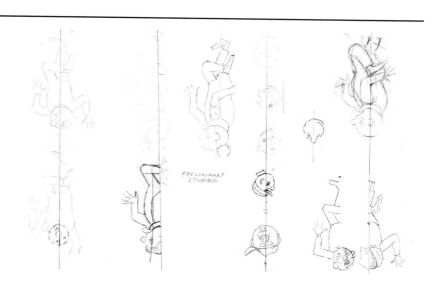

even within the parameters of humorous work, color contrivances can destroy the total effect you're striving for. In the case where varied elements fold together to form a face, flesh tones are flesh tones. How many times can you get away with painting green faces?"

The more he thought about the complications a color Fold-In would create, Jaffee all but conceded the feature had run its course. But when Gaines informed him that, like the front and back covers, the rate of pay for full color art was three times that of black-and-white cover art, Jaffee had second thoughts about giving up the feature so quickly. He responded with a "let's see if it can be done" attitude. Rising to the challenge, Jaffee solved the complexities of a color Fold-In, and has continued to do so for just about every issue of *MAD* since.

Only on several occasions over the years, when editorial needs demanded the use of the inside back cover, did the Fold-In *not* appear in the magazine—much to the disappointment of its loyal readers. In rare cases such as this, the negative

5. Once I have a workable moshing figure, I start composing the overall picture. I split the moshing figure in two and place one part on the left and the other on the right of an enlarged Fold-In grid. A sheet of translucent tracing paper goes over the page, and I fill in the center section.

6. On a new sheet of tracing paper I refine and tighten the details of the completed drawing.

response wasn't totally ignored by *MAD*'s editors, who quickly made sure the next issue contained Jaffee's beloved creation.

"How does Jaffee do it issue after issue for all these years?" remains the most frequently asked question about the Fold-In. And it's asked more often by *MAD* editors than by *MAD* readers! How he does it *mechanically* is explained by the accompanying graphics below. How he does it *creatively* is another matter altogether, perhaps explained only by Jaffee's masterful visual sense of design and composition. Using form, color, and a distorted perspective as *deception* more than accurate *depiction*, he manipulates those elements available to him.

Each Fold-In is in reality two separate entities. The initial work addresses the editorial question posed for that particular piece, while the subsequent folded version graphically supplies the editorial solution to the puzzle.

The principal image is composed of four separate sections, each measuring one-quarter of the total width, with a quarter on both the left and right sides and a half in the center section. When the right quarter is folded over to meet the left quarter, the middle half disappears and

7. To work out the final details of the finished illustration, I cut the middle section out and match the left and the right sections to each other.

8. After corrections are completed on the folded image, the two sections are separated and moved back to their left and right positions.

Photo by Irving Schild

Photo by Irving Schild

a new image is formed.

Jaffee explains, "I could do ten of these a day if the big picture didn't have any connection with the answer. The tricky part is having a connection. In order for the copy to read correctly after it's folded, there has to be a marriage of some sort."

The accompanying text of a Fold-In is a particular brainbuster to write, since the words have to make sense both before and after folding. While not quite as difficult for him to solve as the visual problem, it's still no piece of cake! Jaffee works and reworks the wording, hammering out the initial concept. After this there is more work on banner headlines and captions until he achieves the clarity, brevity, and deception that a Fold-In must have in order to succeed. Jaffee has often relied upon the technical ingenuity of both Al Feldstein, *MAD*'s editor at the time of the first Fold-In, and my co-editor, John Ficarra, who has had that particular responsibility of the feature since 1985.

Each Fold-In begins with a clean slate. Jaffee, a New York City resident, meets regularly with the editorial staff to discuss the current scene, events, trends, and fads. As *MAD* staffers represent the total political spectrum—

9. The previously removed middle part (from 7) is now reinserted and integrated with the left and right sections.

Photo by Irving Schild

conservative to liberal and everything in between—nothing and no one escapes its satirical scrutiny. As might be expected, of the countless ideas tossed about by this iconoclastic group, a high percentage are not fit for publication. But the ideas that do make it to the second round of discussion are still missing the most important aspect of the process—the visual presentation. Many strong statements are just that, word gags that can't be turned effectively into visual gags. They have to be discarded and the whole process started again. Even a master like Jaffee finds a large number of verbal concepts impossible to translate successfully into pictures. Eventually a workable solution is reached and the process of visual mechanics begins once again. (Perceptive readers may have noticed that in Jaffee's caricature of himself, his hair has been thinning over the years; it would be safe to surmise that this is in some small part due to the difficulties of creating the Fold-In.)

MAD's satirical content is met by a necessary—although limiting—"premise approach," which applies to the Fold-In as well. There is a vast difference between subject matter and idea. A case in point might be a writer's suggestion, "How about doing something about the postal service?" That is only subject matter. "How about doing something about the *slowness* of the postal service?" is specific subject matter, but still not an idea. "How about an article showing MAD's suggestions for *speeding up* the postal service?" Now

10. Key background figures are sometimes worked on separately, as I refine their features and size. After finalizing my sketches of Dr. Kevorkian and Alfred E. Neuman, I fit them into the middle section. The completed drawing is then transferred to illustration board.

we're getting closer, but the "idea" still exists in the realm of subject matter. The premise, or "hook" is missing. "Why not show that by turning the postal service against its own workers we can ensure a speeding up of delivery?" is a viable hook, a satirical slant from which hopefully eight or ten strong examples might be derived. One example: Pay all postal service employees by checks that are delivered through the mail. That'll get 'em moving! There you have subject-to-premise-to-humorous-resolve.

The Fold-In is developed through a similar process, albeit in a much more difficult format. Here, the premise is more an observation or perception about a certain political or social phenomenon. The emphasis centers more on the fake-out and visual statement than on a belly-laugh gag. Ideas don't come fast or easy either, often taking Jaffee the *writer* longer to conceive and create than it takes Jaffee the *artist* to execute in his painting.

Jaffee explains, "Being visually oriented, I never thought of myself as a writer. I had no goals or ambitions in the writing area; I just traveled what I considered the normal route for an aspiring young cartoonist—I loved making funny pictures! And what's a funny picture if not a reflection of life, an image with a humorous slant? There were no words in my early attempts, only actions and situations. They either worked or they didn't. The ones that did became samples of *artwork*, nothing else. But when prospective clients laughed and asked, 'Who wrote the gag?' (which was very confusing since I didn't realize that any writing had taken place; I mean, writers used typewriters, smoked pipes, wore scarves—right?) my response was '*I* did, sir.' When enough clients said, 'Oh, then, you're *a writer,* too!' I took their word for it. Who was I to argue with prospective employers?"

M #349

WHAT SUICIDAL FORM OF
ACTIVITY WILL SOON
PUT DOCTOR KEVORKIAN
OUT OF A JOB?

WHAT IS FAST REPLACING
DOCTOR KEVORKIAN AS
THE NUMBER ONE FORM
OF ASSISTED SUICIDE?

WHAT FORM OF ASSISTED
SUICIDE IS NOW GIVING
KEVORKIAN STIFF
COMPETITION?

MOS	T PEOPLE WHO CONSIDER SUICIDE HAVE AC PAIN THAT SIMPLY WON'T GO AWAY. BUT LATELY HEALTHY ONES ARE DOING IT.	HING
MOS	FEW PEOPLE LOOK UPON SUICIDE AS A OUT OF PROBLEMS. BUT SOME WHO'RE TLY NUTS ARE ENGAGING IN THIS VERY T	HING
MOS	PAINFUL ILLNESS USED TO BE THE FORE- T REASON FOR SUICIDE. NOW CRAZIES ARE AC TO GET THEMSELVES OFFED JUST FOR FUN	HING

To find out where assisted suicide is flourishing without doctor K's help, fold page in as shown.

11. Each Fold-In asks a question, which is answered by the text underneath once the picture is folded. It's important to have just the right number of characters per line, which in the early Fold-Ins I composed on graph paper. Now that I work on a computer, it's much easier.

12. Before painting begins, I compose a preliminary rough diagram to determine how the values of light and shadow should fall.

Al Jaffee's formal art training took place in New York City's famed High School of Music and Art. At the time, the curriculum concentrated on the fine arts and included little if any training in the area of commercial art. There were no courses for a would-be cartoonist then, so Jaffee did this part all by himself. He is a self-taught cartoonist, and feels he was one from birth. As a little boy he would spend hours copying the Sunday comics pages from the newspapers, beginning his apprenticeship in the same way as countless others before and after him.

Upon graduating from high school, Jaffee turned down a scholarship to the Art Students League. He knew what he wanted to do, so he went right into the world of professional cartooning instead. He worked for Stan Lee at Timely/Marvel Comics for a number of years, first as an artist/writer, then an associate editor, and finally turning out teenage comic books doing both art and script. Many of Jaffee's other humorous attempts found their way into a variety of comic publications at the time. His loyal followers remember such early features as "Inferior Man" with fond appreciation.

In 1955, a former high school classmate, the enormously talented Harvey Kurtzman (*MAD*'s creator and first editor), asked Jaffee if he'd like to do occasional work for *MAD*. Jaffee jumped at the chance. He didn't, however, become a member of "The Usual Gang of Idiots" until 1958—a dubious

Photo by Irving Schild

13. A quick color sketch helps to establish the overall focus of attention.

14. Photocopies are used to experiment with color. I also do a folded version in color to make sure the focus of attention works in favor of the solution as well.

distinction he's been delighted with ever since.

Over the years, Al Jaffee has become one of the magazine's hallmark artists and writers. His "Snappy Answers to Stupid Questions" spawned dozens of books (selling millions of copies), and his articles, parodies, and gags have countless imitators and fans. However, it is the Fold-In for which he is best known, emulated in episodes of *The Simpsons*, as well as in print ad campaigns for Absolut Vodka and Sennheiser electronics, among others. Steven Spielberg, long a *MAD* fan, prominently used the Fold-In concept when he produced the 1985 film *The Goonies*. In the beginning the kids are seen reading *MAD*, a setup for a later payoff (in the original shooting script) that involves the discovery of a map, which—when folded, Jaffee style—leads them to a hidden pirate's treasure. (No such luck with the Fold-Ins included in this volume, I'm afraid.)

Jaffee was honored by the National Cartoonist Society for his Fold-In and given a Special Features Award at their annual Reuben Awards ceremony. I had the good fortune of being present at that occasion and remarked in typical *MAD* fashion, "Good thing they're giving you the award tonight, Jaf. By next year you'll have run out of ideas and the feature will be dead and buried!"

"I hope so," he responded with the famous Jaffee twinkle in his eyes.

Just for the record, the year was 1972!

Nick Meglin
MAD Co-editor
January 1997

15. The actual artwork is painted in watercolors. Since I don't have the luxury of folding the illustration board, I have to constantly check to make sure the colors on the right side will match perfectly with the colors on the left.

—Al Jaffee

MAD is often asked why it doesn't have expensive full-color three-page fold-outs the way other high-class magazines like "Life" and "Playboy" have. There are two reasons for this! One: MAD is against ostentatious, snobbish, status-seeking gimmicks, and Two: MAD is cheap! So here instead is our economy-minded black-and-white one-page

MAD FOLD-IN

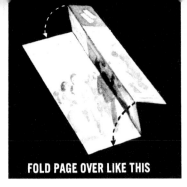

FOLD PAGE OVER LIKE THIS

FOLD THIS SECTION OVER TO LEFT   **FOLD THIS SECTION BACK TO RIGHT**

Elizabeth Taylor, looking **radiantly** beautiful at the **premiere** of her latest film, is positively enchanted by

escort Richard Burton, who glows in the knowledge that he is the only one in her heart, and that she is his.

Meanwhile, people push and shove for autographs while police try to keep them in check! Hey! Take a look at

the handsome young stranger in the crowd moving in for his chance. Obviously, he's destined to be next in line.

No. 86, April 1964

In this first Fold-In (April 1964), the concept was fairly simple. The aim was to make fun of fancy fold*outs* in other magazines. There was little effort here to hide the answer with tricky artwork and text, as in subsequent Fold-Ins. At the time no one expected there would be a second Fold-In, much less this collection. This scene depicts the highly publicized extramarital affair of celebrities Elizabeth Taylor and Richard Burton. (Note the position underfoot of Eddie Fisher, Ms. Taylor's husband at the time.)

Elizabeth Taylor, looking radiantly beautiful at the premiere of her latest film, is positively enchanted by the handsome young stranger in the crowd moving in for his chance. Obviously, he's destined to be next in line.

MAD FOLD-IN

Someone here wants to be President of The United States more than anyone else in the whole wide world. Can you guess who it is? Well, all you have to do is fold this page in (as per directions) and see

WHO WANTS TO BE PRESIDENT MORE THAN ANYTHING?

FOLD THIS SECTION OVER TO LEFT   FOLD THIS SECTION BACK TO RIGHT

FOLD PAGE IN LIKE THIS

RICH CANDIDATES ROCKEFELLER AND GOLDWATER WOULD FIGHT HARD
IN ANY PRE-CONVENTION DEBATES, WEAKENING UNITY, SO
NIXING IDEA WAS BEST FOR PARTY'S CHANCES TO BEAT JOHNSON

Time and time again, he has insisted to the Press that he is absolutely positively not interested in becoming

involved in any inter-party mudslinging. So says Barry, refusing to meet and debate with Rocky. He feels such a

debate would tend to expose weakness in the Republican Party, and hurt either of their chances of becoming

President. However, people close to him—who know him intimately — claim that this is far from the real truth!

SPECIAL SPRING ISSUE
MAD

No. 87, June 1964

The Republican convention in 1964 featured a battle royale between conservative senator Barry Goldwater and moderate governor Nelson Rockefeller for the party's presidential nomination.

But the real story was the young super-ambitious politician lurking in the shadows who hoped they'd knock each other off, thus advancing his own chances in the future. Unlike the first Fold-In, this one tries to hide the answer with deceptive artwork and text.

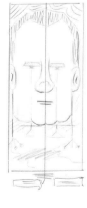

RICHARD

NIXON

Time and time again, he has insisted to the Press that he is absolutely positively not interested in becoming

President. However, people close to him—who know him intimately — claim that this is far from the real truth!

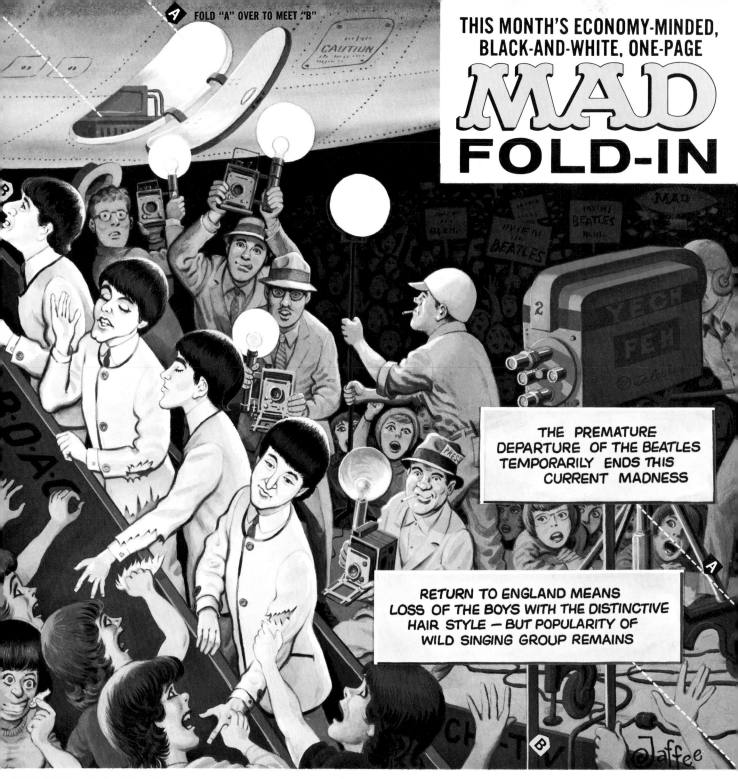

THIS MONTH'S ECONOMY-MINDED, BLACK-AND-WHITE, ONE-PAGE

MAD
FOLD-IN

THE PREMATURE DEPARTURE OF THE BEATLES TEMPORARILY ENDS THIS CURRENT MADNESS

RETURN TO ENGLAND MEANS LOSS OF THE BOYS WITH THE DISTINCTIVE HAIR STYLE — BUT POPULARITY OF WILD SINGING GROUP REMAINS

THE ONLY HOPE FOR CURING "BEATLE-MANIA"!

Revealed by the MAD FOLD-IN

The Beatles came and went, leaving the U.S.A. a shambles. Now they're back in England, making movies...while grave concern grips both nations and the rest of the world. But there's still hope! To find out what can save us all from this "Beatle-Mania," merely fold page in diagonally as shown in the box on the right.

FOLD IN PAGE DIAGONALLY LIKE THIS

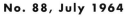

No. 88, July 1964

The Beatles phenomenon hit the United States in 1964 with their arrival in New York. Young people here responded with the same enthusiasm that this exciting group generated in Britain. Older people thought this was just another short-lived teenage craze. Long hair, rare among males at that time, was ridiculed by many who were not ready to be caught up in this Beatles worship. As you can see, I was still experimenting with the form; this was the only time the Fold-In folded in the unusual manner shown here.

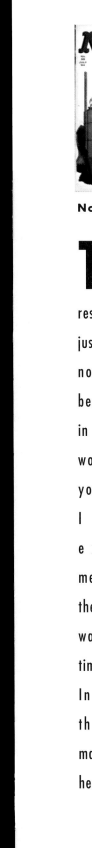

FOLD "A" OVER TO MEET "B"

THIS MONTH'S ECONOMY-MINDED, BLACK-AND-WHITE, ONE-PAGE

MAD FOLD-IN

CAUTION

PREMATURE LOSS OF THE BEATLES HAIR ENDS THIS WILD MADNESS

HERE WE GO WITH ANOTHER CLEVER, WITTY AND RIDICULOUS
MAD FOLD-IN

The recent national election was one of the roughest, dirtiest and mudslingingest in history. Each political party accused the other of the worst things possible, and everyone took a beating, regardless of whether he won or lost. Now we should try to bind up the wounds. If you fold page in as shown, you'll discover...

FOLD IN PAGE LIKE THIS

WHICH NATIONAL SYMBOL IS GOING TO NEED THE BIGGEST REPAIR JOB?

A ▶   FOLD THIS SECTION OVER LEFT   **◀ B**   FOLD BACK SO "A" MEETS "B"

THE BITTER PUNISHMENT THAT THESE TWO GREAT AMERICAN
POLITICAL SYMBOLS TOOK IS NOW MAKING
EACH WINCE WITH PAIN AT THE SLIGHTEST WIGGLE

No. 94, April 1965

Even back in 1964, elections were pretty negative. The contestants were Republican Barry Goldwater and Democrat Lyndon Johnson. The main issue was the Vietnam war. Although President Johnson was increasing American involve-

ment daily, it wasn't enough for superhawk Goldwater. The Democrats used the issue in a vicious television ad campaign, implying Goldwater would use nuclear bombs if elected. As always in a dirty campaign, the only one really battered was our nation's image.

THE AMERICAN

EAGLE

No. 118, April 1968

Interesting historical note (maybe!). Unbeknownst to me, this was the last Fold-In to be done in black and white. Although color was coming to the inside back cover, that meant nothing in this Fold-In. The only color the patients

in this scene are concerned about is the color of *money*. *Lots of it.* Escalating hospital bills were scaring the pajamas off every person unfortunate enough to need hospitalization. Even those with insurance were facing bankruptcy when long stays, due to so-called catastrophic illness, were sending their bills into the stratosphere. By comparison, today's hospital bills are into another universe altogether.

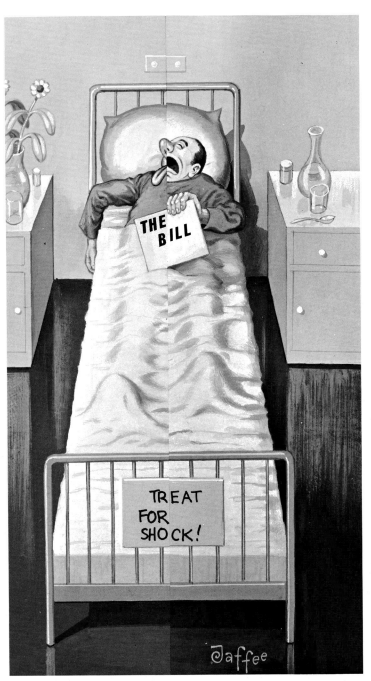

GETTING
THE BAD
NEWS

HERE WE GO WITH ANOTHER RIDICULOUS
MAD FOLD-IN

Spring is the time of year when our thoughts turn to the soil and "Spring Planting." And when it comes to planting, many people have "Green Thumbs." But there is one dedicated group of people who do a lot of planting, and yet nothing ever comes up. To find out who these people are, fold in the page as shown.

FOLD PAGE OVER LIKE THIS!

A▶

FOLD THIS SECTION OVER LEFT

◀ B FOLD BACK SO "A" MEETS "B"

THE UNSUCCESSFUL AMATEUR GARDENER, IN SO MANY CASES, IS THE ONE WHO FAILS TO FIND OUT ABOUT SOIL CONDITIONS BEFORE A VEGETABLE OR FLOWER SEED IS PLANTED.

A▶

◀B

No. 119, June 1968

This was the first color Fold-In (see Introduction for the story behind this move). It was scheduled to appear in the spring, so I figured what better way to showcase color than with a gardening scene.

I played around with a number of ideas featuring flower beds, bouquets, etc., without success. Later, a news story broke about the Mafia and something called the "Cosa Nostra." It tied them to a number of unsolved killings. The word "planting" popped into my mind and the Fold-In was on its way.

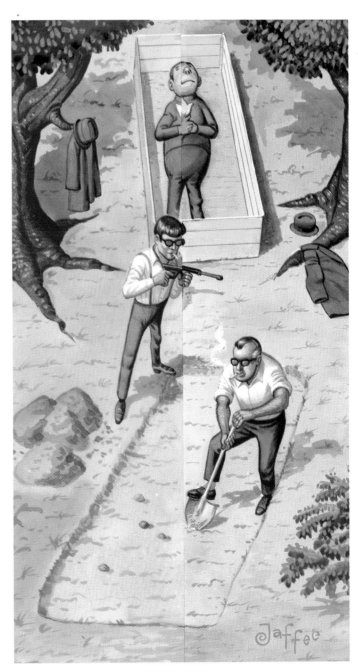

THE MA-

FIA

WHAT IS THE ONE THING PROTEST MARCHES HAVE GREATLY IMPROVED?

HERE WE GO WITH ANOTHER RIDICULOUS
MAD FOLD-IN

Almost every day, there is a Protest March being held somewhere, demanding one thing or another. Most of the time, these marches have little effect, due to the callousness and lethargy of our legislative represent-atives. However, there is one area where Protest Marches have had fantastic results, and improvements have been phenomenal. To find out what it is, fold page in as shown:

FOLD PAGE OVER LIKE THIS!

A ▸   FOLD THIS SECTION OVER LEFT   ◂ B   FOLD BACK SO "A" MEETS "B"

SHOVING, SHOUTING PROTESTERS PARADE
THEIR SIGNS AND BANNERS AS THEY
SALLY FORTH DAILY IN ENDLESS DROVES

A ▸   ◂ B

No. 125, March 1969

The no-win Vietnam war dragged on interminably, and antiwar sentiment was steadily increasing. By 1969 it was reaching fever pitch, and

anger against our leaders spilled over to other issues, resulting in a variety of protest demonstrations almost daily.

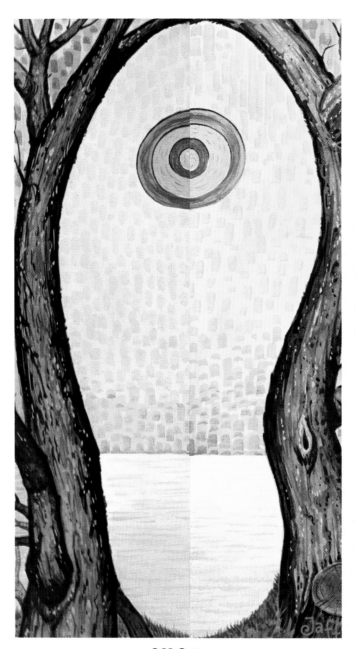

SHOE

SALES

THAT CHASM KNOWN AS THE "GRAND CANYON," ONCE
GENERALLY ACCEPTED AS THE GREATEST NATURAL CREATION
GOD DEVISED, IS NOW MERELY A DENT ON THE MAP
COMPARED TO THIS NEWLY-DISCOVERED FAULT

A ▶   ◀ B

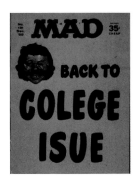

No. 131, December 1969

Another outgrowth of the Vietnam protest era was the recognition that a certain previously undefined "chasm" existed in our world. Suddenly, it seemed  one generation became aware that another generation was recklessly sending it off to die for reasons that were never clearly explained. Awareness of the "generation gap" was thrust into the open.

**THE
GENERATION
GAP**

HERE WE GO WITH ANOTHER RIDICULOUS
MAD FOLD-IN

Conservationists are constantly screaming about one or another species of American fauna that is threatened with extinction. But one such creature is fast disappearing and few people seem to care. To find out what animal this is, fold in page as shown.

FOLD PAGE OVER LIKE THIS!

A ▶   FOLD THIS SECTION OVER LEFT   ◀ B   FOLD BACK SO "A" MEETS "B"

THOUGHTFUL PEOPLE ALL THROUGH THE U.S.A. DEPLORE
WANTON DESTRUCTION OF ANIMAL LIFE. BUT IF EVER
HAVOC BEFELL THIS HATED PEST, THEY WOULDN'T SQUAWK

A ▶   ◀ B

No. 134, April 1970

This Fold-In of April 1970 relates to Vietnam. After 350,000 American casual-

ties, the public's appetite for this pointless war was diminishing. The prowar "hawks," who had dominat-ed for many years, were beginning to drift into the ranks of the peace-loving "doves." Suddenly, the cry of the "warhawk" was no longer being heard as loud. This reality, along with the fact that certain bird and animal species were becoming extinct, helped the Fold-In to work.

**THE
WAR
HAWK**

HERE WE GO WITH ANOTHER REVOLTING

MAD FOLD-IN

The dangers of inflation are apparent to us all. But there is one insidious form of inflation that is far more dangerous than the rest, and has occupied the minds of millions of Americans for years. Fold in page as shown to find out what it is!

FOLD PAGE OVER LIKE THIS!

A▶   FOLD THIS SECTION OVER LEFT   ◀B FOLD BACK SO "A" MEETS "B"

HOUSING UP 223%

TRANSPORTATION UP 198%

FEDERAL, STATE, & LOCAL INCOME TAXES UP 157%

CLOTHING UP 112%

REAL ESTATE, SCHOOL, SALES & LOCAL TAXES UP 178%

HOME FURNISHINGS UP 212%

GROCERIES UP 174%

APPLIANCES UP 127%

OIL   SOAP   FLOUR

INSURANCE UP 106%

ENTERTAINMENT UP 133%

SERVICES UP 163%

MEDICAL COSTS UP 464%

EDUCATION UP 237%

PAY CHECK

Jaffee

GENERALLY, ALL THE ATTEMPTS AT COMBATTING INFLATION IN THIS ONE AREA HAVE FAILED TO PUT AN EFFECTIVE STOP TO IT

A▶   ◀B

MAD 35¢

IN THIS ISSUE:
BOTCH CASUALLY AND
THE SOMEDUNCE KID

No. 136, July 1970

In 1970 two forms of inflation were beginning to worry people. One was economic. The other was personal. This Fold-In was particularly tricky

because the figure in the folded version had to come out of a lot of strange objects. In later Fold-Ins, I tried to avoid this "seemingly obvious" type of solution.

GETTING

FAT

HERE WE GO WITH ANOTHER REVOLTING
MAD FOLD-IN

As usual at this time, stores and catalogues are filled with millions of Christmas goodies. But there's one essential item we could all use, and it looks like it won't be available again this year. To find out what this one gift is that we all long for and need desperately, fold in page.

FOLD PAGE OVER LIKE THIS!

A▶   FOLD THIS SECTION OVER LEFT   ◀B FOLD BACK SO "A" MEETS "B"

A▶   ◀B

No. 140, January 1971

Almost every Christmas, it seems, some intensely desired item is in short supply. This Fold-In pretends that the item is a  consumer product. The answer is something quite different. This is the first time Alfred E. Neuman features in a Fold-In. Also, in the background are two little military figures. They are based on another  ongoing feature that I was doing in *MAD* at the time, one titled "Hawks & Doves."

MAJESTIC SURROUNDINGS NEITHER GUARANTEE NOR MEAN SAFETY. EVERY NEWSPAPER AND PERIODICAL EXPOSES DAILY OUTRAGES THAT OFFEND OUR SENSES

A▶   ◀B

No. 153, September 1972

This is the first Fold-In that experiments with a multipanel sequence. The implied "assault" in the headline plays off the increasing violence in our society.

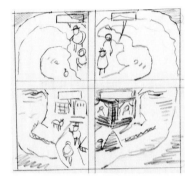

After folding, we discover that the "assault" is not on our person but on our pocketbooks. At the time, many major medical problems were not covered by insur-ance, and the result was— and still is—bankruptcy for many families.

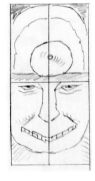

**MAJOR
MEDICAL
EXPENSES**

WHAT EMERGING FORCE THINKS IT IS CLEVERLY SOLVING THE PROBLEM OF OVERPOPULATION?

HERE WE GO WITH ANOTHER RIDICULOUS
MAD FOLD-IN

Although the "Over-Population Problem" has been growing more acute through the years, a previously unheard-from force has only recently emerged from obscurity, claiming (among other things) a unique solution to this serious crisis. To discover their previously unheralded answer to the Population Explosion, fold in the page as shown.

FOLD PAGE OVER LIKE THIS!

A▶ FOLD THIS SECTION OVER LEFT   ◀B FOLD BACK SO "A" MEETS "B"

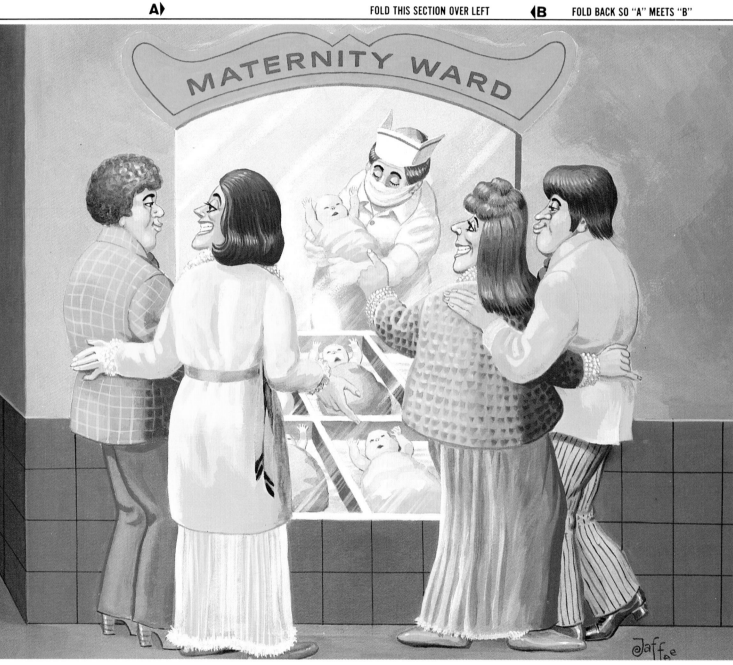

MATERNITY WARD

GAZING ADORINGLY AT BRAND NEW OFFSPRING IS PRETTY EXCITING FOR RICH PARENTS. BUT FOR MANY MORE POOR ONES, FEWER BABIES MIGHT BE THE HAPPIER ANSWER

A▶   ◀B

No. 166, April 1974

In 1974 there was a great deal of public discussion regarding the dangers of world-wide over-population. At the same time there was a gay rights move-

ment, and people began coming out of the closet. When I brought this Fold-In idea to *MAD*'s editorial staff, some concern was expressed. Fortunately, "political correctness" had not yet been invented and I got the go-ahead. I won them over by saying, "If we can't view serious matters with a bit of whimsy, we might as well all quit and hide in a closet."

GAY

POWER

WHAT KIND OF VICIOUS BIG SHOTS HAVE BEEN TAKING OVER OUR CITIES?

HERE WE GO WITH ANOTHER RIDICULOUS
MAD FOLD-IN

One "Big Shot" after another has always tried to muscle in on crowded, troubled cities! But lately, a most vicious and dangerous type has emerged to threaten the urbanite. To discover the identity of this new menace, fold in page.

FOLD PAGE OVER LIKE THIS!

A▶   FOLD THIS SECTION OVER LEFT   **◀B** FOLD BACK SO "A" MEETS "B"

ARTIST & WRITER: AL JAFFEE

SATURATED WITH POWER, THIS NEW "BIG SHOT" HAS A HEYDAY NETTING MILLIONS FROM HELPLESS VICTIMS WHOSE PLIGHT SPECIFICALLY AMUSES THE BIG SHOT'S MORBID VICIOUS PALS

A▶   **◀B**

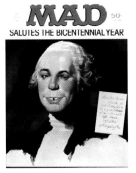

MAD 50¢
SALUTES THE BICENTENNIAL YEAR

No. 181, March 1976

Street crime took on a new wrinkle in 1976. Cheap handguns, known as Saturday night specials, were flooding our inner cities. It didn't matter that some states had strong

antigun laws. The Saturday night specials were easily brought in from states that had few, if any, laws against the sales of these weapons. Naturally, with the low price tag these guns commanded, they became especially popular with teenage gang members. Though it made them feel like "big shots," the real big shots, as the folded picture shows, were the guns themselves.

CITY SEWER

@Jaffee

**SATURDAY
NIGHT
SPECIALS**

WHAT'S THE BEST THING TO USE TO SEE STARS?

HERE WE GO WITH ANOTHER RIDICULOUS
MAD FOLD-IN

Interest in Astronomy has grown immensely in recent years. But one new device has helped a lot of people see stars that they never knew existed. To find out what that new device is, fold in the page as shown:

FOLD PAGE OVER LIKE THIS!

A▶   FOLD THIS SECTION OVER LEFT   ◀B   FOLD BACK SO "A" MEETS "B"

A SKILLED STARGAZER CAN GATHER SCIENTIFIC MATE-
RIAL ONLY WHEN HE'S PROPERLY EQUIPPED.
BOUNDLESS PATIENCE ALSO HELPS IN THIS REGARD.

A▶   ◀B

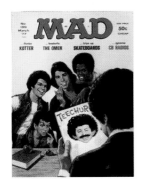

No. 189, March 1977

Skateboard sales were soaring big time in 1977 when this Fold-In was done. So were injuries related to this sport. Unfortunately, as usual, safety equipment came along only after a great many injuries were sustained. Helmets, pads,  guards, wrist braces, etc., eventually became available, but not before thousands of skateboarders were injured. In 1977, for example, 385,000 emergency room visits were made by kids who did not buy safety equipment. Apparently, they felt that saving money was more important than saving their necks. This Fold-In shows one such hapless 'boarder "seeing stars" without the benefit of a telescope.

A SKATE-

BOARD.

WHAT DOES A COLLEGE EDUCATION PROMISE TO GIVE MANY OF TODAY'S STUDENTS?

HERE WE GO WITH ANOTHER RIDICULOUS
MAD FOLD-IN

No one can predict what the future holds for today's college students, but if things keep going the way they're going, then there's one sure thing many of them will get! To find out what it is, fold in page as shown on the right.

FOLD PAGE OVER LIKE THIS!

A▶   FOLD THIS SECTION OVER LEFT   ◀B   FOLD BACK SO "A" MEETS "B"

YOUNG PEOPLE SEEKING A HIGHER STANDARD OF LIVING
BANK ON COLLEGE TO HELP ACHIEVE IT. STUDENTS WHO INTERRUPT
THEIR EDUCATION TO SEEK GOOD JOBS SOON FIND IT'S
PARTICULARLY DIFFICULT WITHOUT "COLLEGE DEGREE" DOCUMENTS

A▶   ◀B

No. 196, January 1978

Parents become petrified with shock when they learn the price of their off-springs' college education. And way back in 1978, the same thing was happening, as some of the MAD staff with

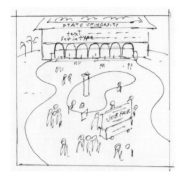

college-bound kids learned. While the big picture in the Fold-In stresses the positive values that the gift of knowledge brings, the folded version shows the "gift" of poverty many parents were experiencing.

BANKRUPT

PARENTS

HERE WE GO WITH ANOTHER RIDICULOUS
MAD FOLD-IN

Actors come from a variety of places, such as neighborhood theaters, summer stock, local TV, repertory companies, etc. But lately, actors are coming from a really unique place. To find out what that place is, fold in page as shown.

FOLD PAGE OVER LIKE THIS!

A▶ FOLD THIS SECTION OVER LEFT   ◀B FOLD BACK SO "A" MEETS "B"

ROYAL CROWN THEATER

THESPIANS TODAY ARE PLAYING EVERYTHING...FROM MACBETH TO LITTLE ORPHAN ANNIE. WHEN SPOTLIGHTS SHINE SHOW FOLKS WORK TIRELESSLY UNTIL THEY REACH THE TOP

A▶   ◀B

No. 199, June 1978

MAD #196 carried a lead story about one of the all-time most popular movies.

MAD's satire was jointly written by Larry Siegal and Dick DeBartolo, with illustrations by Harry North, Esq. It was a smashing spoof of *Star Wars.* I enjoyed their piece so much I decided to do something on *Star Wars* too. The Fold-In pictured here came out several issues later.

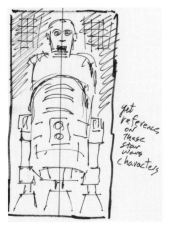

**THE
MACHINE
SHOP**

HERE WE GO WITH ANOTHER RIDICULOUS
MAD FOLD-IN

Hardly anyone today can escape the excitement and impact of the spectacular of professional sports. But our young people are particularly impressed and inspired by the wild goings-on in this great American industry. To find out exactly what the youth of our nation is learning from it, fold in page as shown on right.

FOLD PAGE OVER LIKE THIS!

A ▶   FOLD THIS SECTION OVER LEFT   ◀ B   FOLD BACK SO "A" MEETS "B"

OUR MAGNIFICENT SPORTING EVENTS GREATLY IMPRESS AND INSPIRE THE DEVOTED YOUNG FANS OF ALL FORMS OF SPORTS

A ▶   ◀ B

No. 208, July 1979

Fans have always wanted to be just like their famous heroes, hitting homers, scoring touchdowns, and dunking baskets. But something else even more important has emerged today, as this Fold-In demonstrates.

In big-time sports, the main goal is not only the pursuit of excellence on the playing field. It is also the pursuit of excellence in the field of wealth through astronomical salaries, commercial endorsements, and autograph sales.

GREED

HERE WE GO WITH ANOTHER RIDICULOUS
MAD FOLD-IN

Every day, we hear of some new threat to our way of life. But on this page, a really big disaster has taken place. To find out what it is, fold in page.

FOLD PAGE OVER LIKE THIS!

A▶   FOLD THIS SECTION OVER LEFT   **◀B** FOLD BACK SO "A" MEETS "B"

NUCLEAR SCARES ARE WITH US ... AND WE ALL HAVE TO FACE IT. ALL OVER THE WORLD, PEOPLE ARE BUSY HOLDING MEETINGS SO THEY CAN QUICKLY PINPOINT AND IDENTIFY ANY POSSIBLE THREAT TO THEIR LIVING AREA!

A▶   **◀B**

No. 213, March 1980

We were on a very short deadline for this Fold-In. In desperation I presented a

couple of tepid ideas to my editors, but the concepts didn't fly.

Finally I said, "I guess this issue of *MAD* will have to go with no Fold-In idea."

A chorus of editors responded, "That's it! Do one on that!"

**NO
FOLD-
IN
IDEA!**

HERE WE GO WITH ANOTHER RIDICULOUS
MAD FOLD-IN

Almost all Travel Ads today seem to feature "Bargain Trips". However, there is still one trip that remains as costly as ever. To find out what that trip is, fold in page as shown.

FOLD PAGE OVER LIKE THIS!

A▶ FOLD THIS SECTION OVER LEFT ◀B FOLD BACK SO "A" MEETS "B"

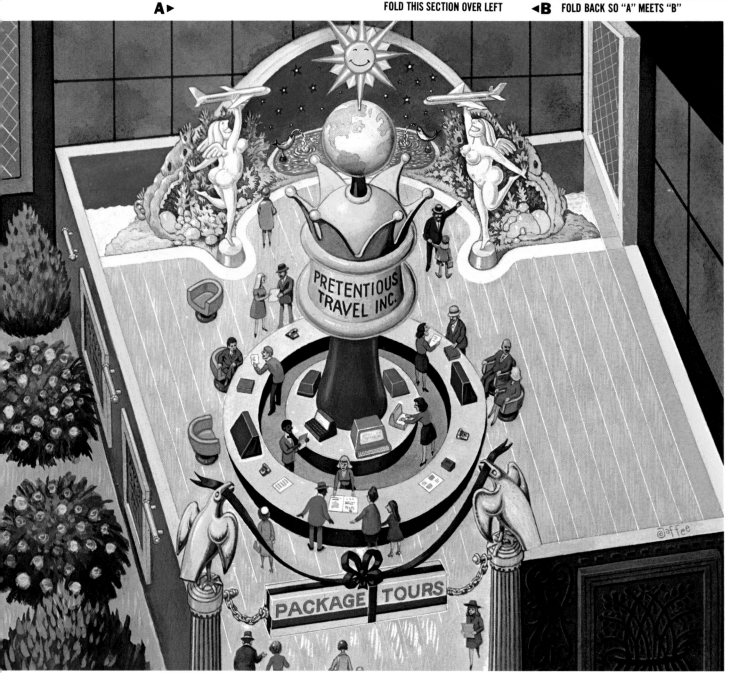

THOUGH BARGAIN TOURS ARE POPULAR, ONE EXPENSIVE LUXURY TRIP IS STILL BEING TAKEN. EVEN THE LEAST OPULENT OF THESE HAS TO COST YOU A SMALL FORTUNE!

A▶   ◀B

No. 220, January 1981

At the time of this Fold-In, news stories were exposing some of the sleazier methods used by undertakers to overcharge people who were too distraught to pay attention. Sometimes, skyrocketing funeral costs caused people to choose cremation in the hopes of saving money. At first this worked fine by eliminating customary funeral charges. But don't grieve for the under-takers just yet. They didn't take this lying down. Little by little they have driven up the cost of cremation with a new set of costs. Now, instead of seeing their savings go into a hole in the ground, the bereaved can watch them go up in smoke.

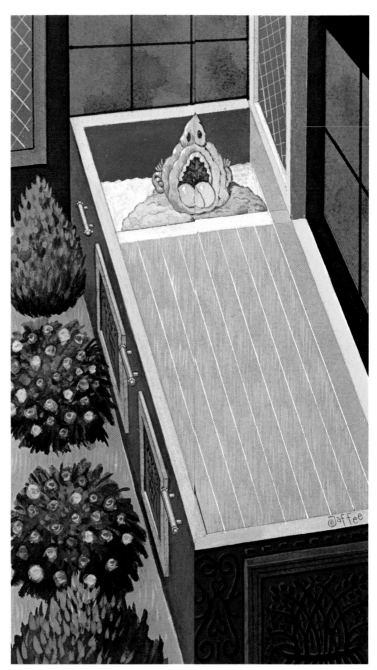

**THE
LAST
ONE!**

HERE WE GO WITH ANOTHER RIDICULOUS
MAD FOLD-IN

Humpty Dumpty fends off some pretty stupid questions in this Mother Goose scene . . . but to get the FINAL SNAPPY ANSWER, you've got to fold in the page as shown at right!

FOLD PAGE OVER LIKE THIS!

A ▸   FOLD THIS SECTION OVER LEFT   **◂B** FOLD BACK SO "A" MEETS "B"

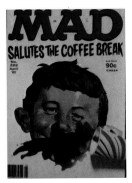

No. 222, April 1981

This Fold-In is based on another feature I created in *MAD* magazine titled "Snappy

Answers to Stupid Questions." (I also wrote and illustrated a number of paperback books on this subject.) Applying this idea to a Fold-In, I had someone ask Humpty-Dumpty a series of stupid questions to which he gives snappy answers. After folding, however, the last laugh is on wise-guy Humpty-Dumpty himself.

SCRAMBLED

EGGS

HERE WE GO WITH ANOTHER RIDICULOUS
MAD FOLD-IN

Each year, Hollywood offers one production that makes everyone's skin crawl. Usually, it is the most horrible thing to come out of "tinsel town" that year. To discover the title of that hideous show for this year, fold in the page as shown . . .

FOLD PAGE OVER LIKE THIS!

A▸   FOLD THIS SECTION OVER LEFT   ◂B   FOLD BACK SO "A" MEETS "B"

THROUGH THE YEARS, HORROR PICTURES HAVE BECOME OFFENSIVE AND DISGUSTING. THESE MOVIES CAN SCAR A YOUNGSTER'S MIND. NO AMOUNT OF MONETARY REWARD SHOULD JUSTIFY ANYTHING THAT SINKS QUITE SO LOW!

A▸   ◂B

No. 223, June 1981

Horror films have been good to Hollywood's bottom line. And sometimes

Hollywood doesn't know when to draw the line before it hits bottom. A case in point—the Academy Awards ceremony. Under all the glitz and hype it is still a dreary, biased, self-congratulatory affair. Although these are exactly the qualities that the *MAD* staff enjoyed, I was able  to persuade them to go ahead with a less-than-flattering Fold-In.

THE OSCAR AWARD SHOW!

WHAT ANCIENT SLOW-MOVING CREATURE IS THREATENED WITH EXTINCTION?

HERE WE GO WITH ANOTHER RIDICULOUS
MAD FOLD-IN

Evolution has taught us that "speed" is one of the elements necessary for the survival of the fittest. Slow-moving creatures have difficulty surviving in a fast-moving world. To find out what the next sad victim of progress could be, fold in page as shown.

FOLD PAGE OVER LIKE THIS!

A▶ FOLD THIS SECTION OVER LEFT **◀B** FOLD BACK SO "A" MEETS "B"

THOUSANDS OF NEW IDEAS HAVE BEEN SUGGESTED TO MAKE POSSIBLE THIS CREATURE'S SURVIVAL, BUT ALL SENTIMENTAL SERMONS ARE WORTHLESS WHEN IT REFUSES TO FOLLOW ADVICE

A▶   **◀B**

No. 225, September 1981

MAD #225, in which this Fold-In appeared, looked normal, but wasn't. Half of it was upside down. Although the Fold-In appeared on the inside back cover, it also appeared on the inside front cover. But that's neither here nor there. The subject of the Fold-In was the threat to both four-legged and two-legged animal life.

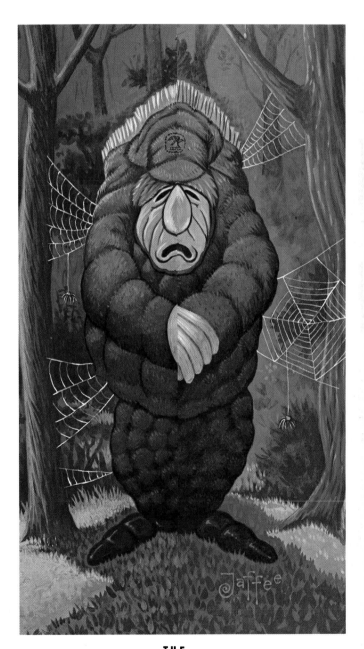

THE
POSTAL
SERVICE

HERE WE GO WITH ANOTHER RIDICULOUS
MAD FOLD-IN

The Chemical Industry has always had to wrestle with the problem of where to dump its poisons. Today, almost every chemical company uses one convenient place to dump toxic products. To find out what that place is, fold in the page as shown at the right.

FOLD PAGE OVER LIKE THIS!

A▶ FOLD THIS SECTION OVER LEFT   ◀B FOLD BACK SO "A" MEETS "B"

IN MODERN LIFE, CHEMICAL TECHNOLOGY PLAYS AN OUTSTANDING ROLE. BUT EVERY INDUSTRIAL PRODUCER BELIEVES THAT THE CHARGES AGAINST HIM ARE JUST LIES INVENTED BY KOOKY ENVIRONMENTALISTS.

A▶   ◀B

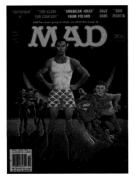

No. 226, October 1981

Every day it seemed like news stories were breaking about deadly chemical discharges into our streams and lakes. At the same time, chemi-cal additives were being pumped into our food. I would have enjoyed doing a Fold-In on how to survive without drinking and eating, but had to settle for a chemical complex turning into staple food items.

ODD SHAPED INDUSTRIAL BLDGS

IN
OUR
BELLIES

WHAT'S THE DIFFERENCE BETWEEN AN IDIOT—AND SOMEONE WHO FOLDS "FOLD INS"?

For years, we've wondered what kind of person actually sits down and "folds" a page so the little "A" meets the little "B." Well, we've found out! And if you want to know too, fold in page as shown.

FOLD PAGE OVER LIKE THIS!

A▶   FOLD THIS SECTION OVER LEFT   ◀B FOLD BACK SO "A" MEETS "B"

TREMENDOUS NUMBERS OF PEOPLE EVERYWHERE IN THE WORLD HAVE FOLDED FOLD-INS. THIS NONSENSICAL ACT REVEALS THEIR TRUE IMAGE

A▶   ◀B

No. 228, January 1982

Normally, the Fold-In is a puzzle of sorts. (No, the puzzle is not why *MAD* publishes it!) A puzzling question is asked in the first picture and the answer comes in the second "folded" picture. But this

particular Fold-In is not a puzzle; it's a riddle. (No, the riddle is not why...oh, forget it!) It is also the only Fold-In that, when folded, comes out the same as it was in its unfolded form.

**THERE
IS
NONE**

HERE WE GO WITH ANOTHER RIDICULOUS
MAD FOLD-IN

The moment you acquired this copy of MAD, you learned how to perform an absolutely fantastic magic trick? To find out what it is, simply fold in the page as shown.

FOLD PAGE OVER LIKE THIS!

A▶   FOLD THIS SECTION OVER LEFT   ◀B FOLD BACK SO "A" MEETS "B"

MAD'S MAGIC IS SO OBVIOUS. EVERYONE FROM HULKING NINCOMPOOPS TO OUTRIGHT GENIUSES IN OUR SOCIETY CAN SEE IT. YOU, HOWEVER, MAY VIEW ITS CONTENTS DISAPPROVINGLY. YOU MIGHT GET SORE AND WANT TO TEAR DOWN THE DASTARDLY MAGAZINE THAT MANIPULATES YOUR BRAIN

A▶   ◀B

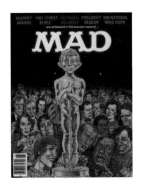

No. 231, June 1982

In 1982 inflation was a serious problem for publishers; their production costs were

rising rapidly. The newsstand price of this issue of *MAD* (#231) was 90 cents, up from 75 cents only a year earlier.

I asked the *MAD* staff if I could make fun of this in the Fold-In. "Sure," they said. To everyone's surprise, *MAD*'s very next issue went up to a dollar, something we didn't know at the time I did this Fold-In.

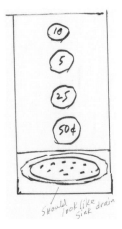

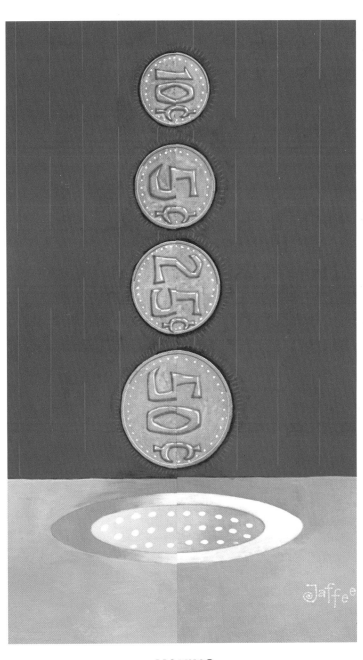

**MAKING
NINETY
CENTS
DISAPPEAR DOWN
THE DRAIN**

WHAT WOULD BE A VAST IMPROVEMENT ON "THE RIGHT TO BEAR ARMS"?

HERE WE GO WITH ANOTHER RIDICULOUS
MAD FOLD-IN

To the chagrin of wildlife lovers everywhere, the Constitutional "right to bear arms" has been used by rifle club members and hunters as their excuse to possess the weapons necessary to carry on their slaughter. For a truly happy and unique MAD solution to the problem, merely fold in the page as shown at the right.

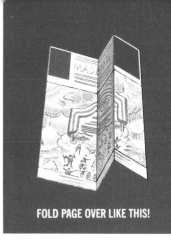

FOLD PAGE OVER LIKE THIS!

A▶   FOLD THIS SECTION OVER LEFT   **◀B** FOLD BACK SO "A" MEETS "B"

THE RIFLE CLUB MEMBER AND HUNTER HAS BEEN TAUGHT TO FIGHT FOR THE RIGHT TO OWN HIS OWN FIREARM BECAUSE LOSING IT IS ONE OF HIS BIGGEST FEARS

No. 235, December 1982

This Fold-In seemed to be on the inside of the *front cover* of the magazine. But that is only because the entire issue was *upside down*. When turned right side up, the Fold-In winds up where it belongs. (No, not the wastebasket—the *inside back cover*.) This Fold-In tweaks the National Rifle Association. Although well known for their playful sense of humor, the NRA was not amused this time. They do not, as a matter of policy, laugh off anything that threatens gun merchants' profits. As a result of this Fold-In, *MAD* received a barrage of hate mail from NRA supporters. Fortunately, it wasn't a barrage of another kind that they are so well equipped to deliver.

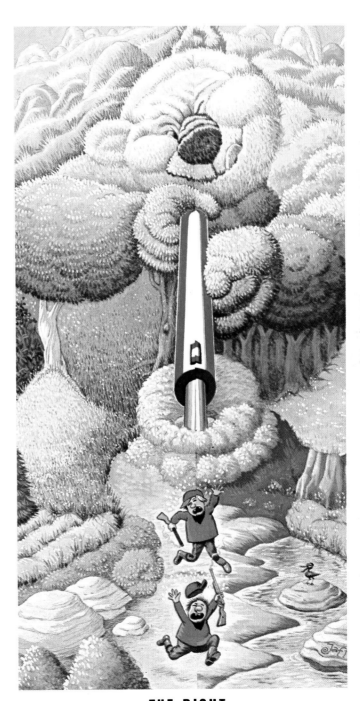

**THE RIGHT
TO ARM
BEARS**

WHAT RECENT SPIRITUAL MOVEMENT HAS (THANK GOD!) BURNED ITSELF OUT?

HERE WE GO WITH ANOTHER RIDICULOUS MAD FOLD-IN

A new spiritual movement that recently swept the country has apparently crashed to earth finally. To find out what spiritual movement we're talking about, fold in page as shown.

FOLD PAGE OVER LIKE THIS!

A▶   FOLD THIS SECTION OVER LEFT   ◀B FOLD BACK SO "A" MEETS "B"

IN THE WORDS OF OUR VERY OWN ALFRED E. NEUMAN..."MANY AN IDIOT HAS JOINED A CULT. WORSE YET, CULTIST LEADERS PROFIT WHEN THEY WHIP SUCH IDIOTS INTO A MONEY-GIVING FRENZY"!

A▶   ◀B

No. 238, April 1983

In 1983, cults of all sorts were spreading like wildfire. Horrifying tales of children

being drawn into their grasp were terrifying parents. Children were disappearing into communes and ashrams, only to reappear at airports in strange clothing and even stranger hairstyles. When found by their parents, these cultists appeared to be in a hypnotic trance. Similarly, an unusual movie hit the screen at this time, starring a gnarled, misshapen, alien

gargoyle from outer space. And with the way children flocked to movie theaters to see *E.T.*, one would think they were all being

brainwashed *en masse*. Blending the two was a perfect Fold-In misdirection.

E. T.
WORSHIP

HERE WE GO WITH ANOTHER RIDICULOUS
MAD FOLD-IN

Despite the fact that prayer in our Public Schools has been declared unconstitutional, the Reagan Administration has decided that it belongs there. To see how they've forced it back in, fold in page as shown at right.

FOLD PAGE OVER LIKE THIS!

A▶   FOLD THIS SECTION OVER LEFT   ◀B   FOLD BACK SO "A" MEETS "B"

BY MAKING SCHOOL PRAYER AN ISSUE, POLITICOS CAUSE TROUBLE. STUDENTS PRACTICE MANY BELIEFS. IT IS ILLEGAL TO USE TAX MONEY FOR FINANCIAL SUPPORT OF RELIGION. PROFESSIONAL LOBBYISTS ARE PAID FOR COLLECTING VOTES SO CONGRESS CAN EFFECT THE LAW'S CHANGE

A▶   ◀B

No. 240, July 1983

  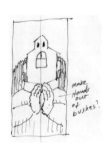

An article of faith in the Reagan administration was to bring prayer back into schools. At the same time, budget cuts for public education were being actively sought. I decided to take a light-hearted jibe at both subjects. Many readers didn't quite see the light part of the jibe. Proponents of school prayer accused us of being against religion. Proponents of student financial aid accused us of being against education. In truth, all I was against was missing the Fold-In deadline.

BY MAKING STUDENTS
PRAY FOR
FINANCIAL AID FOR
COLLEGE

INTEREST IN "HORROR FILMS" IS GROWING THROUGHOUT THE WORLD. WE MUST MAKE SURE CARE IS TAKEN TO STORE THESE CLASSICS IN A SAFE PLACE FOR FUTURE FILM FANS.

A▶   ◀B

No. 241, September 1983

In 1983, the movie industry hit a new high in horror movies. Or should we say a new "low"? Movies displayed every revolting aspect of dismemberment, disembowlment, decapitationment, and painful paper cuts. Some of the goriest blockbusters in a long list were: *The Dead Zone, Halloween III, Amityville 3-D, Cujo, Psycho II, Videodrome,* and something called *Microwave Massacre.* Motion picture codes advising parents on what is not suitable for children are difficult to monitor. In cases where children were not allowed into theaters on their own, many duped idiot adults to escort them inside. Naturally, we of the do-gooder Fold-In brigade could do no less than expose this seamy business. Unfortunately, that resulted in an equally disgusting-looking Fold-In. We hope this can be forgiven as it is in the service of a worthy cause.

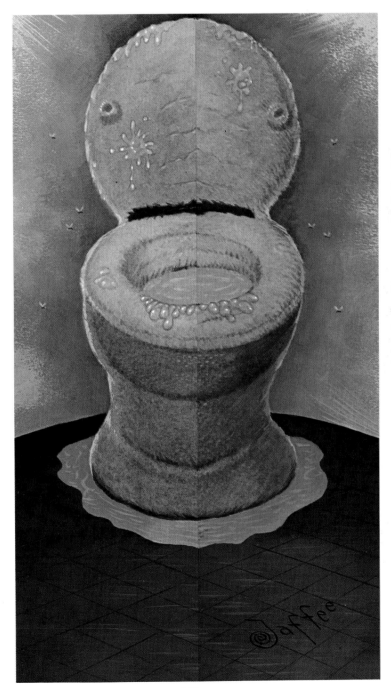

IN
THE
CAN

HERE WE GO WITH ANOTHER RIDICULOUS
MAD FOLD-IN

When peoples of other countries think of America's national symbol, they no longer picture the Bald Eagle! To find out what they *DO* think of, fold in page as shown.

FOLD PAGE OVER LIKE THIS!

A▸

FOLD THIS SECTION OVER LEFT

◂B FOLD BACK SO "A" MEETS "B"

THE BALD EAGLE'S ALWAYS BEEN THE NATIONAL BIRD OF THE U.S.A. BUT THE FEELING AMONG MANY FOREIGNERS IS THAT NOW THIS SYMBOLIC ROLE BELONGS TO ANOTHER FAMOUS THING.

A▸   ◂B

No. 248, July 1984

Americanisms have always been popular with those abroad. But one thing in particular was spreading fast all over the world. Was it the big

sound of rock 'n' roll? Was it the big blockbuster movie? Was it the big breakthrough in science? *No!* It was something *even bigger* than all that. It was the spread of cholesterol as McDonald's Golden Arches were exported to every corner of the globe.

**THE
BIG
MAC**

WHAT GROUP DISPLAYING DEVIANT SEXUAL BEHAVIOR DID THE MEESE COMMISSION OVERLOOK?

HERE WE GO WITH ANOTHER RIDICULOUS
MAD FOLD-IN

The Meese Commission left no bed unturned searching for sexual deviants. But they missed some! You'll have to fold in this page (gasp!) to find out who they are.

FOLD PAGE OVER LIKE THIS!

A▶   FOLD THIS SECTION OVER   ◀B FOLD BACK SO "A" MEETS "B"

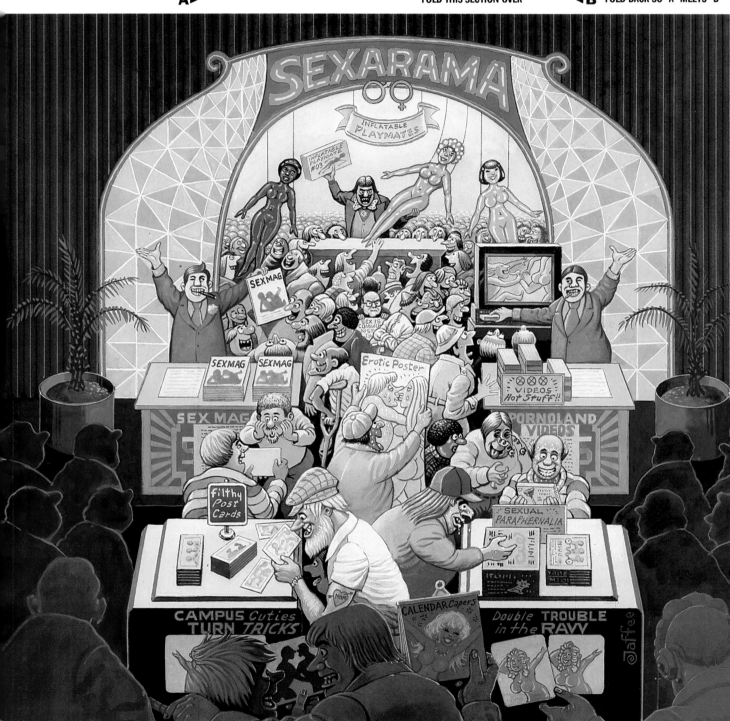

TV WAS EXAMINED BY THE COMMISSION, AS WAS EVERY OTHER FIELD OF COMMUNICATION. ARRANGEMENTS WERE MADE TO COMPILE EXTENSIVE LISTS OF SEXUAL ACTIVITIES THAT MEESE DISLIKED

A▶   ◀B

No. 274, October 1987

This is one of the few inside *front* cover Fold-Ins. (Not like the phony ones in *MAD* #225 and #235.) A great deal of concern was generated about how to fold

this Fold-In. Would it go from A to B or from B to A? Anyway, after it was published, *MAD*'s publisher had bigger problems. A group of goody two-shoes in the Midwest were horrified at the sight of nude inflatable dolls. They threatened supermarkets with a boycott, causing thousands of copies of *MAD* to be bounced. Yours truly thought he and his Fold-In would be folded too, but fortunately the publisher, Bill Gaines, hated self-appointed censors and backed me all the way.

TV
EVANGE-

LISTS

Fearsome predators spend hour after hour looking for prey. When one of them discovers a likely victim, he attacks viciously.

A ▶   ◀ B

No. 275, December 1987

In mid-1987 I was wracking my brain for a Fold-In idea when my wife, Joyce, came

into my studio. "There's a big demonstration on our block," she said, "and the fur is going to fly." "What demonstration?" I asked. "An antifur protest," she replied. I ignored this lousy attempt at humor only because it triggered the Fold-In on this page.

Fur lovers

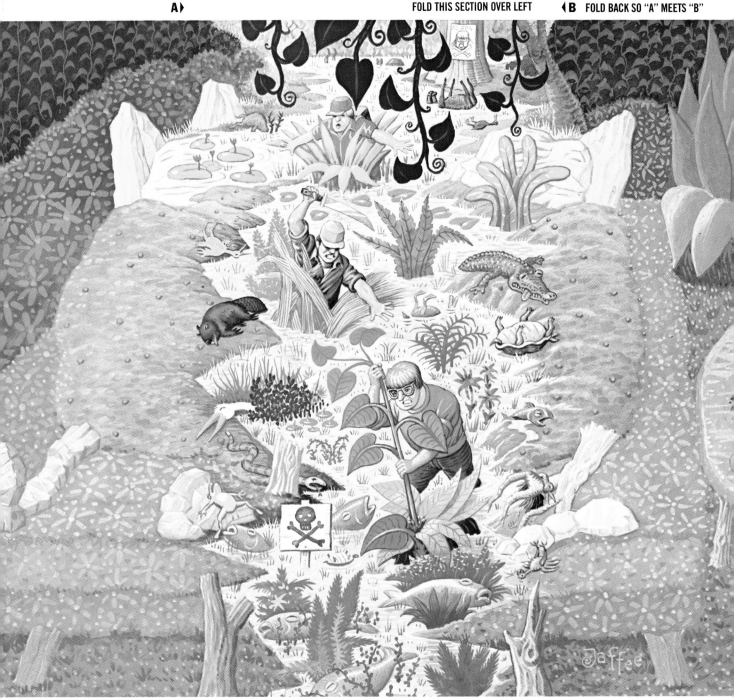

THE COUNTRYSIDE IS BECOMING OVERRUN WITH TOO MUCH WORTHLESS GROWING MATTER. AS STREAMS OF POTABLE WATER ARE CHOKED DRY, ALL LIFE HAS TO EITHER MOVE OR DIE MISERABLY OF THIRST.

A▶   ◀B

No. 280, July 1988

Originally the idea that I presented to *MAD*'s editors for this Fold-In showed the vegetable section of a supermarket, which, when folded, turns into a "couch potato."

They thought the general idea was fine but they were cool to the supermarket setting. Editor Nick Meglin felt it was somewhat contrived and suggested a junglelike scene of rotting vegetation. Everyone agreed, and back to the drawing board I went to create the new middle section shown here.

THE COUCH

POTA TO

HERE WE GO AGAIN WITH ANOTHER
MAD FOLD-IN

Passing or failing is a way of life in school. To find out the latest in this never ending business, fold the page as shown in the diagram on the right.

FOLD PAGE OVER LIKE THIS!

A ▶   FOLD THIS SECTION OVER LEFT   ◀ B   FOLD BACK SO "A" MEETS "B"

THE METHODS USED IN GIVING EXAMS VARY GREATLY. SPECIAL DE-TERRENTS AGAINST CHEATING ARE USED. THE INSTRUCTOR TELLS STUDENTS TO USE TIME WISELY TO SCORE THE BEST

A ▶   ◀ B

No. 288, July 1989

There was a time when the six o'clock news carried reports of one scourge after another in our society. One was kids bringing guns to school. Another was airplanes being hijacked by terrorists. By exposing these horrors in the Fold-In, we tried to alert our readers to the dangers that lurk in the unlikeliest corners of our world and help in some small way. Turning off the six o'clock news could be the start.

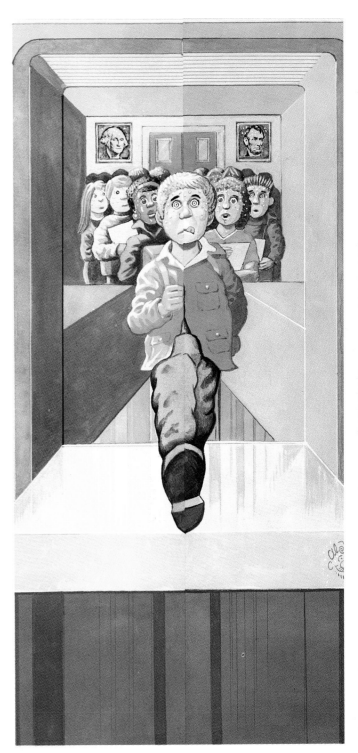

**THE METAL DE-
TECTOR
TEST**

WHAT CREATURE RECENTLY BECAME COMPLETELY EXTINCT IN ALASKA?

HERE WE GO WITH ANOTHER RIDICULOUS MAD FOLD-IN

One creature totally disappeared in the recent Alaskan oil spill. To find out which one it was, fold page in as shown.

FOLD PAGE OVER LIKE THIS!

A ▶

FOLD THIS SECTION OVER LEFT

◀ B   FOLD BACK SO "A" MEETS "B"

THE EXPERTS AGREE—POLLUTERS SHOULD NOT BE EX-
ONERATED WITHOUT FIRST MAKING AMENDS.
CLEARLY, EVERY THINKING YOUNGSTER AND GROWNUP
WORRIES THAT OUR PLANET'LL GET MUCH BLEAKER
AS LIVING CREATURES DIE AND DISAPPEAR.

A ▶   ◀ B

No. 294, April 1990

In 1989 an oil tanker, the Exxon *Valdez*, spilled 240,000 barrels of crude oil into the Gulf of Alaska, killing countless creatures in the area. The particularly alarming aspect

of this story was the snail-paced progress of the cleanup. I was dying to hit Exxon for their inept handling of this environmental disaster, but I just couldn't nail it down. I called *MAD* editor John Ficarra and explained my problem. He loved the idea and said, "How about making the rare creature a cleanup worker?" That was it. Problem solved. (Oils well that ends well.)

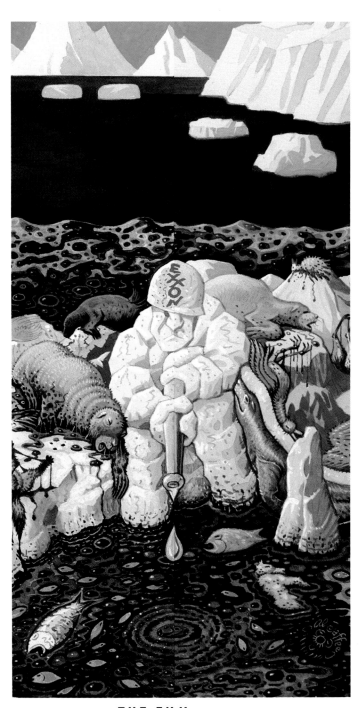

THE EXX-
ON
CLEANUP
WORKER

HERE WE GO WITH ANOTHER RIDICULOUS

MAD
FOLD-IN

FOLD PAGE OVER LIKE THIS!

A ▶   FOLD THIS SECTION OVER LEFT   ◀ B   FOLD BACK SO "A" MEETS "B"

A ▶   ◀ B

No. 295, June 1990

I wish I could say that the idea of a Fold-In based on "Snappy Answers to Stupid Questions" was back by popular demand. So I will. But actually, when I'm down to the last minute of a deadline I'll use any

device I can to get the Fold-In into the pipeline. Cigarette smoke, an ill wind that blows no one good, is always a safe target. I don't mean to be "holier than thou" or preachy, but I'm just happy to expose evil things in our society whenever I can. In fact, one of the evil things is right here in this Fold-In.

Crass commercialism. Note the title of the book casually placed in the hands of the man in bed, and you'll see what I mean.

WHAT MASTER UNDERACHIEVER HAS UNDESERVEDLY ATTAINED WORLDWIDE FAME AND FORTUNE?

HERE WE GO WITH ANOTHER RIDICULOUS
MAD FOLD-IN

Underachievers are never expected to succeed. But despite this, one ne'er-do-well has gained worldwide acclaim. To find out who he is, just fold in page as shown in diagram on the right.

FOLD PAGE OVER LIKE THIS!

A ▶   FOLD THIS SECTION OVER LEFT   ◀ B   FOLD BACK SO "A" MEETS "B"

OUR MINDS ARE SURELY BOGGLED BY THE WORLDWIDE RENOWN OF A CERTAIN UNDERACHIEVER. HE HIT THE FINANCIAL JACKPOT AND INSPIRED EVERY NITWIT WHO'S BEEN BLUFFING HIS WAY THRU LIFE. AS A ROLE MODEL FOR EVERY GOOF-OFF IN THE WORLD HE TAKES FIRST PLACE

A ▶   ◀ B

No. 300, January 1991

This Fold-In is a major leap forward in sneaky deception. Most people who haven't anything better to do than fold Fold-Ins always try to guess what it is. They do this by folding but not folding, visualizing what

the left and right sides will be when combined. I decided to have some fun with these readers by making obviously clear two halves of Bart Simpson's head. But the sneaky part is Bart's head disappears in the centerfold and a completely different picture appears. Who says you can't fool all the people *all* the time?

OUR OWN
AL
JAFF-

EE

WHERE IS OUR GOVERNMENT MOST SUCCESSFULLY USING THE CAMOUFLAGE TECHNIQUE?

HERE WE GO WITH ANOTHER RIDICULOUS
MAD FOLD-IN

The camouflage technique is now used all over the world. But our leaders are using it extremely well in one area. To see how, fold in page as shown.

FOLD PAGE OVER LIKE THIS!

A ▶ FOLD THIS SECTION OVER LEFT

◀B FOLD BACK SO "A" MEETS "B"

HIDEOUS CAMOUFLAGE COLORS ARE USED FOR SIMULATING THE HODGE-PODGE SHADES THAT ARE IN NATURE. THIS TIMELESS PROCESS HELPS ANIMALS SURVIVE. MAN, HOWEVER, IS O-BLIGED TO USE IT AS PART OF HIS WARMAKING SYSTEM.

A ▶   **◀B**

No. 307, December 1991

The Gulf War "blitzkrieg" went like clockwork. It was fast, efficient, and unfinished.

("Saddam is doing just fine, thank you.") Compared to Vietnam, however, this media-less war was a glorious success. The nightly television newscasts showed the marvels of a scientifically engineered war. Foreign correspondents, instead of being someplace foreign, were in the Pentagon briefing room being told how the war was going. Casualties were not shown or discussed. It was a Super Bowl kind of war.

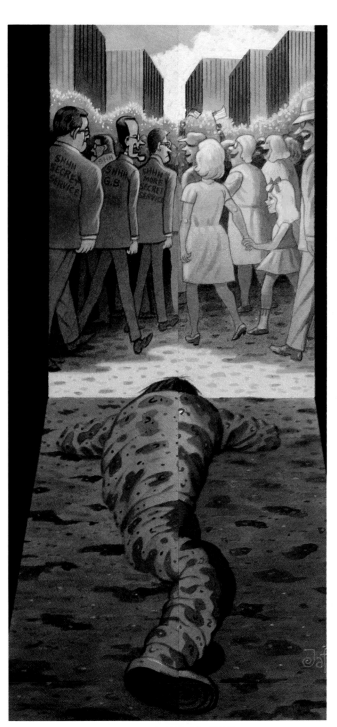

HIDING THE HOMELESS PR O-BLEM.

WHO WAS REALLY THE VICTIM IN A HIGHLY PUBLICIZED SEXUAL HARASSMENT CASE?

HERE WE GO WITH ANOTHER RIDICULOUS
MAD FOLD-IN

Not too long ago charges of sexual harassment made every headline. To find out who the true victim was, simply fold page in as shown.

FOLD PAGE OVER LIKE THIS!

A ▶   FOLD BACK SO "A" MEETS "B"   ◀ B   FOLD THIS SECTION OVER LEFT

PEOPLE DISAGREE A LOT ABOUT SEXUAL CRIMES. THE WOMAN'S VIEW IS OFTEN IGNORED BY MEN. THEY SEE HER AS A SEDUCTRESS WHO'S OUT TO ENSNARE EVERY MAN

A ▶   ◀ B

No. 310, April 1992

Think Fold-In is a good example of misdirection. Sexual harassment was in the news. It was natural to suspect a female would be the victim here. The surprise answer (HOOHAH!) was a *man*! Pee Wee

Herman was caught with his pants down. As a result, it was bad news for Pee Wee—his TV show was canceled, his career stumbled, his income nose-dived. But the worst humiliation of all was still to come—his appearance in this Fold-In!

PEE
WEE
HERMAN

WHAT'S THE ONLY WAY FOR TODAY'S YOUTH TO INSURE THEIR FINANCIAL STABILITY?

HERE WE GO WITH ANOTHER RIDICULOUS
MAD FOLD-IN
To find out how young people today are securing their lives, simply fold page as shown in the diagram to the right.

FOLD PAGE OVER LIKE THIS!

A▶   FOLD THIS SECTION OVER LEFT   ◀B FOLD BACK SO "A" MEETS "B"

MORE AND MORE OF TODAY'S YOUNG PEOPLE ARE HAVING BASIC JOB PROBLEMS. MANY OF THEM MUST PICK HIGHLY PRACTICAL WAYS TO LIVE ON A LOW INCOME

A▶   ◀B

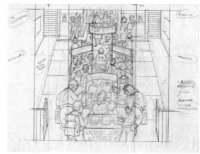

No. 313, September 1992

This was an era when both jobs and affordable housing were scarce. Young people who had moved out of their parents' homes were having a very tough time of it.  They had left behind the comfort of family life with few responsibilities. Pop paid the rent and utility bills while Mom picked up the dirty dishes and clothing. The strain of surviving was taking a terrible toll. Was this happening to a great many youngsters? No! It was happening to a great many *parents* when kids started moving back home.

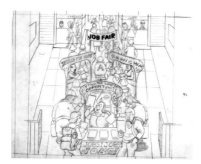

MOVING
BACK
HOME

WHAT'S THE MOST EFFECTIVE WAY TO DEAL WITH REPEAT OFFENDERS?

HERE WE GO WITH ANOTHER RIDICULOUS MAD FOLD-IN

These days, certain shifty and sleazy criminals take advantage of the ins and outs of the law. To find out how to put an end to this, simply fold in page as shown in diagram to the right.

FOLD PAGE OVER LIKE THIS!

A▶ FOLD THIS SECTION OVER LEFT   ◀B FOLD BACK SO "A" MEETS "B"

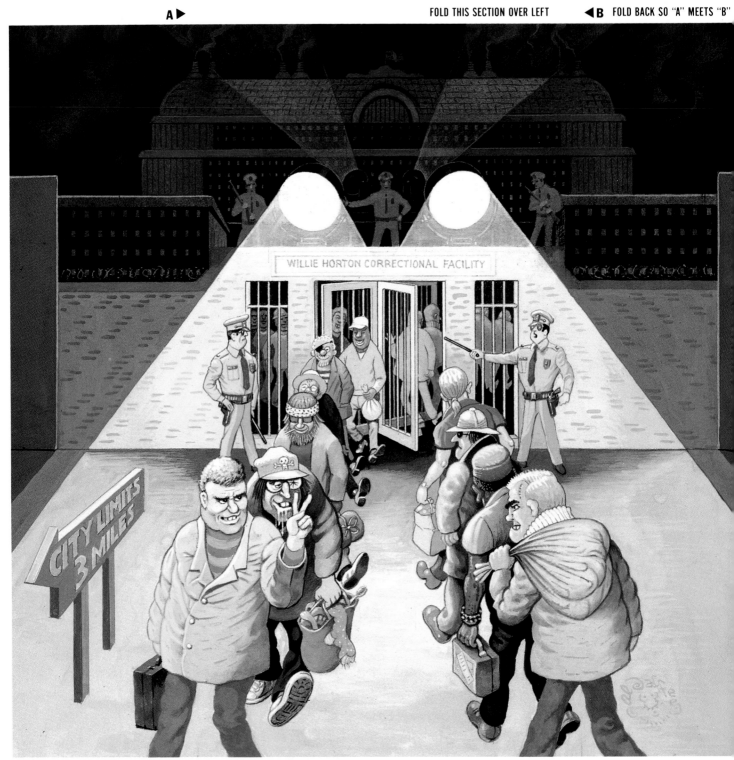

DOES OUR SYSTEM TRAIN CROOKS SO THEY DON'T RE-ENACT THEIR LIVES OF CRIME? NO! WE NEGLECT THEM AND THEN PAY FOR IT WITH HIGHER TAXES

A▶   ◀B

No. 315, December 1992

This Fold-In was scheduled to appear in the 1992 election issue of *MAD*. As in every previous election, crime was high on the campaign agenda. What particularly incensed voters was the notion of *revolving-door justice*, in

which criminals were furloughed for good behavior, committed another crime, and were sent back to prison. However, a number of recent news stories pointed out that not all crime was perpetrated by these criminals. This Fold-In revealed that the revolving door works just as well for crooked politicians.

DON'T
RE-ELECT
THEM

WITH THE DEMISE OF THE SOVIET FLEET, WHAT APPEARS TO BE OUR NAVY HOTSHOTS' LATEST TARGET?

HERE WE GO WITH ANOTHER RIDICULOUS
MAD FOLD-IN

To find out what our Navy's up to in this fast changing world, simply fold in page as shown in the diagram to the right of page.

FOLD PAGE OVER LIKE THIS!

A▶   FOLD THIS SECTION OVER LEFT   ◀B FOLD BACK SO "A" MEETS "B"

FLEET COMMANDERS OF THE U.S. NAVY FACE RE-MARKABLE NEW CHALLENGES. SINCE THERE'S LITTLE OFFENSE LEFT IN THE RUSSIAN NAVY. OUR TACTI-CAL PLANNERS MUST NOW FOCUS ON OTHER DANGERS

A▶   ◀B

No. 316, January 1993

This Fold-in plays up the heroic image of the navy. The setting is a formidable-looking military war room. The impression is clearly one of the dedicated professional naval personnel doing their American duty with pride and precision. Their military

bearing and snappy uniforms add mightily to their Superman-like aura. The folded version, however, focuses less on the

uniforms and more on the ordinary bozos with raunchy ideas of fun who are wearing them. The Tailhook scandal tarnished the navy brass more than any number of military misadventures they might experience.

FE-
MALE
OFFI-
CERS

No. 320, July 1993

The July 1993 issue of *MAD* is the one and only time the Fold-In was featured on the front cover. It was personally gratifying for me to list and showcase all the *MAD* friends and colleagues I've admired through the years. Though they seem to be sufficiently acknowledged on *MAD's* masthead as "The Usual Gang of Idiots," I feel a bit more should be added. They are, by far, "The Most Unusual Gang of Super Talents" to me. To this day it's a pleasure, a privilege, and a great learning experience to know and work with them.

HERE WE GO WITH ANOTHER RIDICULOUS
MAD FOLD-IN

These days America's families are taking a beating everywhere they turn. Housing, transportation and education costs are staggering. There's one area, however, where the family has been particularly hard hit. To find out where, simply fold page in as shown.

FOLD PAGE OVER LIKE THIS!

A ▶   FOLD THIS SECTION OVER LEFT   ◀B FOLD BACK SO "A" MEETS "B"

FOR THE AVERAGE PERSON NOTHING IS AT A BARGAIN PRICE. WHEREVER HE GOES HE WILL PAY THROUGH THE NOSE AND FEEL LIKE A JERK

JURASS-HAS-HAD-IT
PARK

No. 323, December 1993

While the average worker's salary remained stagnant during this period, his expenses were steadily rising. There was only one way to escape and forget money worries. Sports! Seeing zillion-aire athletes make zill-ions of dollars every time they step out to play is very relaxing. On the other hand, that joy is shortlived. The cost of attending an athletic event can land your bank account in last place.

HIGH COST OF TICKETS $

DRINKS

&

FOOD

AT A
BALL
PARK

WHO ON TV
IS SURPASSING
RUSH LIMBAUGH
FOR INTELLECTUAL
SOCIAL
COMMENTARY?

HERE WE GO WITH ANOTHER RIDICULOUS
MAD FOLD-IN

Rush Limbaugh is a TV hit due to his thought-provoking right wing
extremist views. But now, Americans are turning to a new source for
views that surpass Limbaugh for wit, originality and intelligence.
To find out what exactly this competition is, fold page in as shown.

FOLD PAGE OVER LIKE THIS!

A ▶   FOLD THIS SECTION OVER LEFT   ◀ B   FOLD BACK SO "A" MEETS "B"

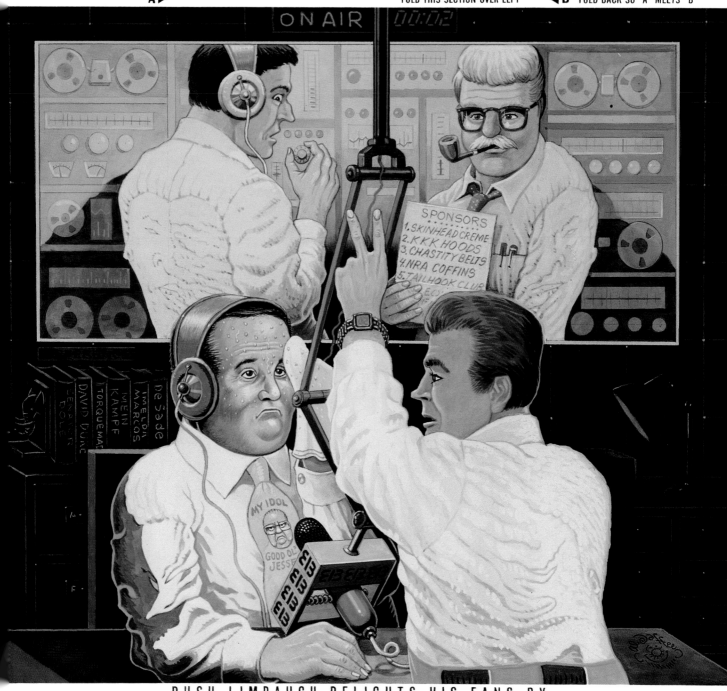

RUSH LIMBAUGH DELIGHTS HIS FANS BY
BEATING UP ON HIS ENEMIES. HIS ENORMOUS IN-
VISIBLE LOYAL AUDIENCE LOVES VENEMOUS HATE AND
BIGOTRY. THEY GET OFF ON ATTACKS THAT'RE' UTT-
ERLY MERCILESS TO LIBERALS, FEMINISTS,
HOMOSEXUALS, AND OTHERS THEY FEAR AND DREAD.

No. 325, February 1994

I called for a conference of *MAD*'s editorial staff to present a hot Fold-In idea. Attending were co-editors Nick Meglin and John Ficarra, art director Jonathan Schneider, associate editors Charlie Kadau and Joe Raiola, assistant editor Andrew Schwartzberg, and intern David Shayne. I presented my idea attacking "shock radio" in which a broadcasting studio morphs into a toilet spewing garbage. To spare my sensitive feel-ings, they answered in chorus, "Why is Jaffee spewing this garbage at us?" No, only kidding. They liked the idea but not the solution. We kicked it around for a while, and the group effort resulted in the Fold-In shown here.

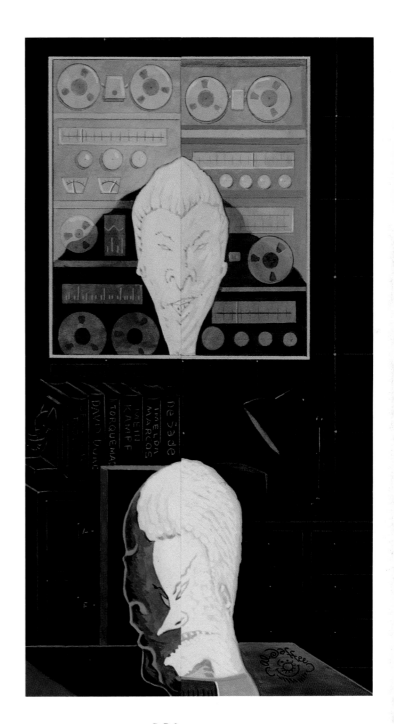

BEA-
VIS AND
B UTT-

HEAD.

WHAT'S EMERGING AS THE GREATEST THREAT TO OUR NATION'S YOUTH?

HERE WE GO WITH ANOTHER RIDICULOUS
MAD FOLD-IN

It is clear to everyone that today's youth has to deal with some pretty horrible things on a daily basis — guns in school, gang warfare, drug dealers and deciding if it's still hip to wear flannel shirts. To find out another horror that plagues our nation's youth daily, fold page in as shown.

FOLD PAGE OVER LIKE THIS!

A ▶   FOLD THIS SECTION OVER LEFT   ◀B   FOLD BACK SO "A" MEETS "B"

ABUNDANT EVIDENCE SHOWS THAT TODAY'S PERMISSIVE SOCIETY IS HARMING OUR CHILDREN. IT IS PARTICULARLY TRAGIC FOR THE YOUNG WHO ARE ENTICED INTO AWFUL ACTS BY CRIMINAL ELEMENTS.

A ▶   ◀B

No. 343, March 1996

Grown-ups in America are deeply concerned about the fate of our youth. They feel kids can't resist the temptation of drugs, sex, and crime. They wish for a return to good old family values.

Unfortunately, some good old family values are what they need to worry about *most.*

ABUSIVE

PAREN-

TS.

WHAT IS FAST REPLACING DR. KEVORKIAN AS THE NUMBER ONE MEANS OF ASSISTED SUICIDE?

HERE WE GO WITH ANOTHER RIDICULOUS
MAD FOLD-IN

Every few months Dr. Kevorkian (AKA Dr. Death) appears in the news either after helping a terminally ill person commit suicide or because he is on trial for his participation. These days, however, Dr. K has some outside competition. To find out how people are killing themselves without Dr. Kevorkian's help, fold page in as shown.

A▶   FOLD THIS SECTION OVER LEFT   ◀B   FOLD BACK SO "A" MEETS "B"

PAINFUL ILLNESS USED TO BE THE FORE-MOST REASON FOR SUICIDE. NOW CRAZIES ARE ACHING TO GET THEMSELVES OFFED JUST FOR FUN

A▶   ◀B

No. 350, October 1996

Dr. Kevorkian has put assisted suicide on the front burner. But there are many forms of assisted suicide that no one pays much attention to. And what's worse, they don't involve terminally ill people. They simply involve "terminally idiotic people."

—Al Jaffee

MOSHING